Withdrawn

STONEFISH
Needles of Pain

by Meish Goldish

Consultant: Brian Nelson, Senior Aquarist
New England Aquarium
Boston, Massachusetts

BEARPORT
PUBLISHING

New York, New York

Credits

Cover and Title Page, © Stephen Frink/Science Faction and © Mark A. Johnson/Corbis; 4, © Pierre Tostee/ZUMA Press; 5, © Mark Conlin/Alamy; 6, © Michaela O'Neill/APN Australian Publishing; 7, © Ippei Naoi; 8, © Roger Steene/Image Quest Marine; 9, © Stephen Frink/Science Faction; 10, © Reinhard Dirscherl/Alamy; 11, © Jack Jackson/Robert Harding Picture Library/Alamy; 12, © Clay Bryce/SeaPics.com; 13, © David Doubilet/National Geographic/Getty Images; 14, © Tom Campbell/splashdowndirect/Peter Arnold Inc.; 15, © Mark Conlin/Visual&Written/Alamy; 17, © Prisma/SuperStock; 18, © David Doubilet/NGS Image Collection; 19, © Stephen Frink/Corbis; 20, © Jurgen Freund/Nature Picture Library; 21, © Reinhard Dirscherl/SeaPics.com; 22T, © Mark Conlin/Alamy; 22B, © Brandon Cole Marine Photography/Alamy.

Publisher: Kenn Goin
Senior Editor: Lisa Wiseman
Creative Director: Spencer Brinker
Photo Researcher: Omni–Photo Communications, Inc.
Design: Dawn Beard Creative

Library of Congress Cataloging-in Publication Data

Goldish, Meish.
 Stonefish : needles of pain / by Meish Goldish.
   p. cm. — (Afraid of the water)
 Includes bibliographical references and index.
 ISBN-13: 978-1-59716-943-1 (library binding)
 ISBN-10: 1-59716-943-9 (library binding)
 1. Stonefishes—Juvenile literature. I. Title.
 QL638.S42G65 2010
 597'.68—dc22

                          2009015489

For more information, write to Bearport Publishing Company, Inc., 101 Fifth Avenue, Suite 6R, New York, New York 10003.
Printed in the United States of America.

10 9 8 7 6 5 4 3 2 1

Contents

A Painful Step

In 2008, Eruch Rowan and a friend were **surfing** off the coast of Australia. After riding a wave, Eruch jumped off his board in a shallow part of the water. His foot landed on something hard and sharp. He looked down and saw that he had stepped on a stonefish—one of the most **venomous** sea creatures in the ocean. The needle-like points on the fish's body had **punctured** his middle toe.

After about 30 seconds, Eruch felt a terrible pain. "It was like a burning sensation, and at the same time a feeling like my foot had been crushed by a sledgehammer," he said later. As the pain grew greater, Eruch knew he needed help fast.

Surfing is a popular sport in the waters off Australia, where Eruch's accident occurred.

Eruch stepped on a stonefish about 11 inches (28 cm) long, similar to the one shown here.

DANGER

When injected into a victim, a stonefish's venom can kill within hours if medical care is not given.

Racing for Help

Eruch got out of the water quickly. He was driven to a nearby building where lifeguard Rob Adsett jumped into action. He placed Eruch's foot in a bucket of hot water to break down and weaken the venom. He also gave Eruch **oxygen**. The great pain caused by a stonefish sting can make victims breathe too quickly and pass out. Giving the victims oxygen helps them control their breathing. Eruch then went to the hospital to be checked by a doctor.

After returning home, Eruch still had a swollen foot and chest pains for days. Yet he was lucky. The emergency treatment he received from Rob had saved his life.

Lifeguard Rob Adsett (left) was able to help Eruch (right) after he was stung by a stonefish.

Even a dead stonefish can pass on its venom to a person who steps on it.

What's in a Name?

Stonefish are among the most **toxic** creatures in the ocean. They're also one of the strangest-looking fish. They get their name from their appearance—they look a lot like stones or rocks. Their bodies have a hard covering that is bumpy and **crusty**. They are usually brown or gray, but many are very colorful and have patches of red, orange, or yellow.

Stonefish vary in size. Most are from 6 to 15 inches (15 to 38 cm) long. However, some can grow as long as 20 inches (51 cm). That's almost as long as some tennis rackets!

Some stonefish can be quite colorful.

A stonefish has a large head.

DANGER

There are 31 different **species**, or kinds, of stonefish.

A Hidden Danger

Since stonefish look like stones, they can be hard to recognize in the water. They often blend into their surroundings on the rocky ocean floor or on colorful **coral reefs**.

Something else also makes stonefish hard to spot—they almost never move. Instead of swimming around like other fish, they lie still most of the time. Their stillness and **camouflage** colors help them hide from enemies and watch for **prey** without being noticed. However, their stone-like looks also make it easy for people to step on them by accident.

Many marine animals do not see stonefish hiding in the water.

stonefish

Stonefish can lie still for days at a time. They are able to stay down on the ocean floor because their bodies don't have **swim bladders** to keep them afloat in the water.

Stonefish blend in easily on the ocean floor.

Unlucky 13

When people step on a stonefish, they are injected with venom that is stored in **glands** under the fish's skin. The venom travels up 13 needle-like **spines** that are on the fish's back. Each spine is covered with flesh. When the stonefish is resting, the spines stay covered. However, if someone touches the fish, the spines rise from their fleshy covers and jab the person's skin. The venom then flows into the victim's body.

a stonefish spine

spines

DANGER
The spines on a stonefish are sharp enough to push through thin shoes and sandals. Each spine holds enough venom to kill 1,000 mice.

Tricky Hunters

Although a stonefish has dangerous spines, it does not use them to catch prey. The fish gets its food in another way. First it uses its front **fins** to dig a hiding place in the sand or mud. Then it lies still, waiting for a meal to swim by. When the prey finally appears, it doesn't see the hidden fish that's ready to spring into action. Before the unlucky animal knows what's happening, the stonefish leaps up, sucks the prey toward its mouth like a vacuum, and swallows it whole. The entire attack takes less than one second!

fin

fin

mouth

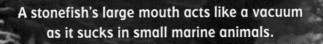
A stonefish's large mouth acts like a vacuum as it sucks in small marine animals.

Due to their toxic venom, stonefish have few enemies. However, sharks, stingrays, and large sea snails will sometimes eat them.

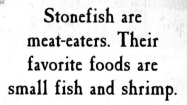

DANGER

Stonefish are meat-eaters. Their favorite foods are small fish and shrimp.

Stonefish Homes

Stonefish live in the warm waters of the Indian and Pacific oceans. Many are found off the coast of China and Southeast Asia, while others live in areas that range from Africa to Australia.

Most stonefish stay in shallow water that's no more than 10 feet (3 m) deep. However, they can be found as far down as 130 feet (40 m). Some lie in mud or sand. Others rest on coral reefs, clinging to rocks that are covered with **algae**.

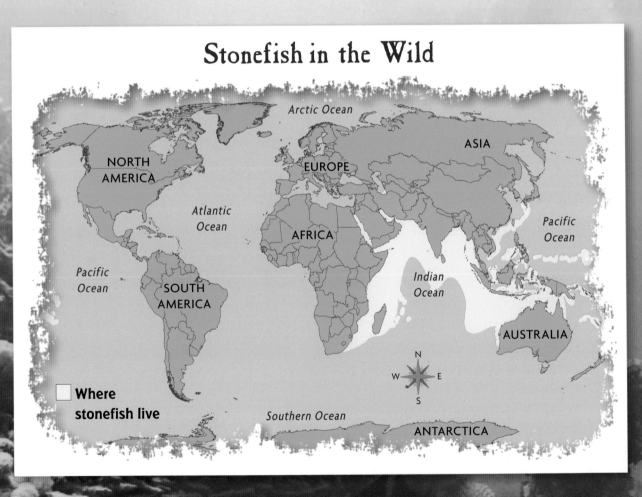

Stonefish in the Wild

Arctic Ocean

ASIA

NORTH AMERICA

EUROPE

Atlantic Ocean

Pacific Ocean

AFRICA

Pacific Ocean

SOUTH AMERICA

Indian Ocean

AUSTRALIA

N
W — E
S

☐ **Where stonefish live**

Southern Ocean

ANTARCTICA

coral reef

stonefish

stonefish

coral reef

Many stonefish blend in with coral reefs because they look like pieces of coral.

Stonefish produce a sticky slime that makes mud and algae stick to their bodies. Along with its camouflage colors and bumpy skin, this helps the animal hide in coral reefs or on the muddy ocean floor.

Baby Stonefish

Adult stonefish usually live alone, meeting other stonefish only when they mate. Once mating has occurred, the female lays a group of jelly-like eggs at night on the ocean floor. Then she hides them in the sand so enemies cannot find and eat them. The babies that hatch from the eggs are strong and well developed. Like their parents, they have deadly venom in their bodies that they are ready to use. So watch out!

A young stonefish

DANGER

A stonefish egg is about .06 inches (1.5 mm) long. That may sound small, yet it is actually larger than the eggs of most ocean fish.

The average stonefish lives five to eight years.

In Case of a Sting

A stonefish sting is very dangerous. If not treated, victims can suffer pain, shock, body swelling, muscle damage, and even death. Experts offer this advice to sting victims.

1. Get out of the water right away. If you pass out in the ocean, you can drown.
2. See a doctor immediately to receive medicine, called antivenom (an-tee-VEN-uhm), that will weaken the venom.
3. If you cannot get to a doctor right away, soak the wound in very hot water for 30 to 90 minutes.
4. Use tweezers to remove any spines from your skin.
5. Scrub the wound with soap and water. Then wash the area with freshwater.
6. Do not close the wound. If you do, you may trap the venom, which can increase pain and damage to the body.

DANGER

If a victim is using hot water to weaken the venom, he or she should make sure the water is not so hot that it burns his or her skin.

Danger Stonefish! protect your feet

It's important to remember not to get too close to a stonefish!

Other Things That Sting

Stonefish are one kind of fish with a venomous sting that can injure or kill its victims. Other kinds of fish also have deadly stings.

Lionfish

- These beautiful and colorful fish are found mainly in coral reefs in the shallow, warm waters of the Indian Ocean, Pacific Ocean, and the Atlantic Ocean.
- Lionfish often swim in pairs. They are not scared away if someone or something approaches them in the water.
- The fish have long, sharp spines that inject venom into an attacker.
- Lionfish injure many divers who accidentally kneel on them or put their hands on them in the water.

Stingrays

- These fish are often found in shallow ocean waters. They are especially active in the summer, when they mate.
- Stingrays do not attack or sting anyone or anything unless they feel they are in danger or are stepped on.
- A stingray generally has one sharp spine on its tail. The spine injects venom into the victim, usually in the foot or lower leg. The sting is quite painful.
- Thousands of people are injured by stingrays each year. People can avoid stepping on them by shuffling their feet as they walk in the water.

Glossary

algae (AL-jee) small plantlike organisms that grow in water or on damp surfaces

camouflage (KAM-uh-flahzh) coloring or covering on an animal that makes it look like the things around it

coral reefs (KOR-uhl REEFS) groups of rock-like structures formed from the skeletons of small sea animals called coral polyps; usually found in shallow tropical waters

crusty (KRUHS-tee) having a hard, bumpy outer layer or covering

fins (FINZ) flap-like body parts on a fish that help it to move through the water

glands (GLANDZ) body parts that produce chemicals

oxygen (OK-suh-juhn) an invisible gas in the air that people need to breathe to stay alive

prey (PRAY) animals that are hunted by other animals for food

punctured (PUHNGK-churd) made a hole by using a sharp object

species (SPEE-sheez) groups that animals or plants are divided into according to similar characteristics; members of the same species can have offspring together

spines (SPINEZ) hard, sharp, needle-like growths on some animals and plants

surfing (SURF-ing) riding the waves in the ocean, usually on a surfboard

swim bladders (SWIM BLAD-urz) bag-shaped body parts found in some fish that hold air and allow them to float

toxic (TOK-sik) poisonous, deadly

venomous (VEN-uhm-uhss) able to attack with a poisonous bite or sting

Index

Bibliography

Burton, Maurice, and Robert Burton. *International Wildlife Encyclopedia* (*Volume 18*). Singapore: Marshall Cavendish (2002).

Cropp, Ben, ed. *Dangerous Australians: The Complete Guide to Australia's Most Deadly Creatures.* Concord, CA: Bay Books (1993).

Tilton, Buck. *How to Die in the Outdoors: 100 Interesting Ways.* Merrillville, IN: ICS Books (1997).

Williamson, John A., Peter J. Fenner, Joseph W. Burnett, and Jacquie F. Rifkin. *Venomous and Poisonous Marine Animals.* Sydney, Australia: University of New South Wales Press (1996).

Read More

Cerullo, Mary M. *The Truth About Dangerous Sea Creatures.* San Francisco, CA: Chronicle Books (2008).

McFee, Shane. *Deadly Fish.* New York: PowerKids Press (2007).

Miller, Sara Swan. *Funny Fishes.* London: Franklin Watts (2000).

Wilkes, Angela. *Dangerous Creatures.* Boston, MA: Kingfisher Books (2007).

Learn More Online

To learn more about stonefish, visit
www.bearportpublishing.com/AfraidoftheWater

About the Author

Meish Goldish has written more than 200 books for children.
He lives in Brooklyn, New York.